The "Reason Why" Books

HOUSES

Irving and Ruth Adler

The John Day Company   New York

THE "REASON WHY" BOOKS

Sixth Impression

© 1964 by Irving and Ruth Adler

The John Day Company, 257 Park Avenue South, New York, N.Y. 10010
an Intext publisher

Published on the same day in Canada by Longman Canada Limited.

Library of Congress Catalogue Card Number: 64-20708
Printed in the United States of America

Contents

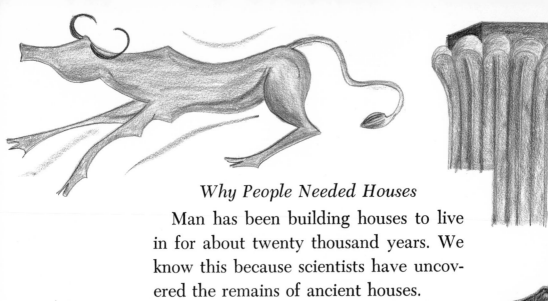

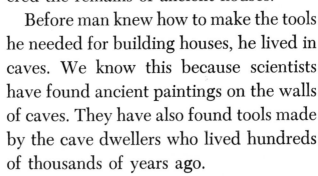

Why People Needed Houses

Man has been building houses to live in for about twenty thousand years. We know this because scientists have uncovered the remains of ancient houses.

Before man knew how to make the tools he needed for building houses, he lived in caves. We know this because scientists have found ancient paintings on the walls of caves. They have also found tools made by the cave dwellers who lived hundreds of thousands of years ago.

Caves and houses are *shelters*.

Man needed a shelter to protect himself against the weather. He did not have a natural coat to protect him against freezing cold. In a cave or a house he could stay warm while it was very cold outside.

Man needed a shelter to protect his fire against the wind and rain. He needed fire to keep him warm and to cook his food. Starting a fire was a hard job, so he kept his fire burning all the time. He could keep the fire from going out in a cave or a house.

Man needed a shelter to protect himself against wild animals. Without a shelter, he was in danger of being attacked while he ate or slept.

Since man built his first shelter, changes have taken place in the things he does to keep himself and his family alive. With these changes, the houses he has built have changed.

This book tells the story of houses from ancient times to the houses people live in today.

Houses like this are built in the hottest parts of Africa. Their thick clay walls keep the heat out.

The Kind of Houses People Build

The kind of houses people build depends on the tools they have. It also depends on the knowledge they have inherited from people who lived before them. We can build skyscrapers because the people who lived 100 years ago learned how to make steel cheaply. The skeleton of the skyscraper is made of steel girders. The huge lifting and digging machines used in construction are made of steel, too. There are people who live today on Pacific

6

islands near Asia whose tools are made of stone and wood. The houses they build are crude huts.

The kind of houses people build depends on where they live. People who live where it is very hot need houses that keep the heat out. People who live where it is very cold need houses that keep the heat in. People who live where there is a lot of rain and snow need houses with sloping roofs. The sloping roof sheds rain and snow. People who live where there are many trees build their houses out of wood. People who live in places where there are few trees use natural building stone, if they can find it nearby. Otherwise they may use pounded mud or bricks. Bricks are artificial building stones made from mud or clay.

The kind of houses people build depends on how they earn a living. People who are hunters build shelters that they use for only a short time. They can build these shelters quickly and do not mind leaving them behind when they move on to a new hunting area. People who are herdsmen build light tentlike houses that they can take down, carry, and set up easily when they move on to a new grazing area. Houses that are used for only a short time or that stay in one place for a short time are called *temporary* houses. People who are farmers, tradesmen and craftsmen build houses that stay in one place for a long time. These are called *permanent* houses.

A hunter who lived 20,000 years ago painted this bull on the walls of the cave in which he lived.

Ancient Hunters' Houses — 20,000 Years Ago

The cave dwellers were hunters. They lived in caves in the wintertime. They could keep themselves warm by building their fires near the cave entrance. In the summertime they were free to move from place to place as they hunted. So in the summertime they lived in temporary shelters that they could build quickly. Such summer shelters were sometimes made of a framework of young tree trunks covered with birch branches and twigs.

There were hunters, too, who lived where there were no caves. These hunters built their own cavelike shelters to live in when it was very cold. First they scooped

8

out the earth, making a large oval hollow. The hunters of England piled the scooped-out earth around the hollow, making an earth wall. They covered the hollow with a roof of branches. The mammoth hunters of Czechoslovakia made a tentlike covering of animal skins over the oval hollow. The hearths in which they built their fires were placed in the middle of the floor.

The mammoth hunters of Russia built shelters that were completely underground. First they scooped out enough earth to make the floor of a shelter eight or nine feet below ground level. They then placed heavy logs over the top of the excavation and covered them over with the scooped-out earth. The hunters used sloping earth paths to enter their shelters. They placed their hearths near the entrance, so that the smoke could escape.

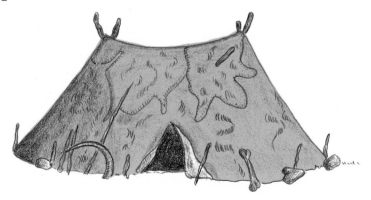

The mammoth hunters of Czechoslovakia built a cavelike shelter which they covered with animal skins.

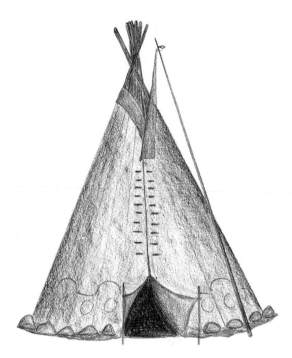

A Plains Indian tepee

Houses of Indian Hunters

The Indians who lived on the Great Plains of North America were hunters, too. The Plains Indians lived in *tepees* (TEE-pees). A tepee was made by first tying together three or four long poles at one end and then standing them up to form a frame. Then fifteen or so more poles were placed so that they leaned against this frame. The whole framework was covered with a carefully fitted buffalo skin. The bottom of the skin was weighted down with stones to keep the wind out. The Indians built their fire near the center of the tepee. The smoke went out through an opening at the top of the tepee. Whenever the Indians moved on to new hunting grounds, it was the job of the women to take down the tepee and set it up at its new site.

The Eskimo is a present-day hunter. In the winter some Eskimos build *igloos* (IH-gloos). An igloo is made of large blocks of dry snow, about 18 inches thick. The Eskimo first makes a large circle of the snow blocks, by placing them end to end. This is the base of the igloo. Then, standing inside the circle, he keeps placing block after block in a spiral, making them slope in a little at the same time. In this way he builds a house shaped like a *hemisphere* (HEM-ih-sfeer) or half ball. Since the Eskimo has been standing inside, he must cut a hole in the wall of the igloo to let himself out. He then builds a low tunnel of snow leading to this hole. The Eskimo enters the igloo by crawling through the tunnel on his hands and knees. Inside the igloo, he builds a snow sleeping platform which he covers with animal skins. He hangs skins across the igloo's entrance and over its walls. Even though an igloo is made of snow, the Eskimo can build a fire inside it.

One reason an igloo works so well as an Arctic house is because of the nature of snow. The snow walls of the igloo lose heat to the cold outside. The inside of the igloo, in turn, loses heat to the snow walls to make up for this

An Eskimo igloo

loss. But snow cannot store much heat so it cannot lose much heat to the outside. So the inside of the igloo has to make up for only a small loss of heat by the snow walls. This is one reason why the inside of the igloo doesn't lose much heat.

The skins that cover the walls of the igloo, and the air space trapped between the skins and the walls, also help to keep the heat in.

A third reason an igloo works so well as an Arctic house is because of its shape. A house loses its heat to the outside through the surface of its walls. An amount of space in the shape of a hemisphere has a smaller surface than the same amount of space would have if it had any other shape. So a house in the shape of a hemisphere loses less heat to the outside than a house of the same size with any other shape.

Each of these solids contains the same amount of space, about 2,400 cubic feet . . .

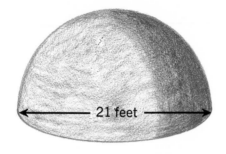

. . . but the hemisphere has about 700 square feet of surface . . .

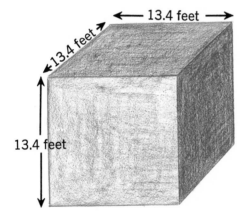

. . . the roof and walls of the cube have about 900 square feet of surface . . .

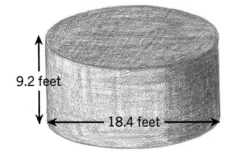

. . . the roof and wall of the cylinder have about 800 square feet of surface.

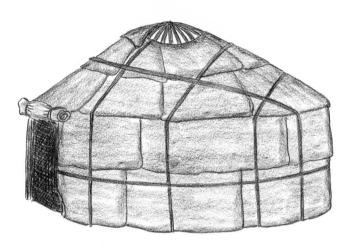

A Mongolian yurt

A Herdsman's House

When people learned how to raise plants and animals they no longer had to hunt. They got their food by farming and herding. Herdsmen had the problem of finding food for their animals. Some herdsmen fed their animals by letting them graze all year round. When the animals had eaten up the grass in one place, the herdsmen moved them to another. These herdsmen had to be always on the move. They had to keep moving their houses, their families, and everything they owned. These wandering herdsmen were called *nomads* (NO-mads). There are still nomads today. They build houses that are easy to take apart, easy to carry, and easy to set up again. The *yurt* of the Mongolian tribesman of Siberia is such a house.

The yurt is a circular hut with a lightweight wooden

The yurt's wooden frame

frame. The frame is made in two parts. The lower part is made of thin slats of wood that crisscross. It can be folded up like a baby's safety gate when the yurt is moved. It is about four feet high and stands upright. Curved poles join the lower part of the frame to a circular wooden ring at the top. The whole frame is covered with large pieces of heavy felt.* Sometimes the inside of the frame is covered with felt, too. The two layers of felt with air trapped between them keep the yurt warm in the same way that the skin-lined walls of an igloo do. A piece of felt is hung over the door of the yurt. It is rolled up when the door is open.

The fire for cooking and for heating the yurt is built in the center of the floor. Smoke goes out through the circular ring at the top of the yurt.

---

* To find out more about felt, read *Fibers*, by the same authors. The John Day Company, 1964.

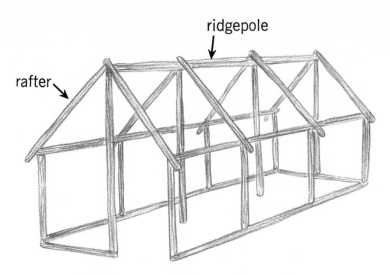

The frame of an ancient farmhouse

Ancient Farmers' Houses

Once people began to plow land and to plant and harvest crops, they no longer had to move as hunters and nomads did. So farmers could build a house in one place and keep it there all the time. Since it did not have to be moved, a farmer's house did not have to be lightweight. So a farmer's house could have more than one room and even more than one floor. It could be made of heavy materials like logs, stone or bricks. The houses that people live in today are descendants of the permanent houses of the first farmers.

Great forests covered Central Europe 6,000 years ago. So the farmers who lived then built their houses of wood. They built their houses in villages for protection. The villages were surrounded by walls of earth and upright

16

logs, and by ditches. The houses were very large. They measured about 30 feet by 100 feet.

To build one of these houses, first three rows of poles were set in the earth. The three rows of poles held up the *rafters* and the *ridgepole*. The rafters and the ridgepole formed the frame of the sloping roof. The house needed a sloping roof to shed rain and snow.

The house was divided into two parts. One part had a raised floor. The walls of the two parts were finished differently. One part had walls of logs that were set upright in the soil. The logs were set one right next to the other. Walls like this are called *stockade* walls. The other part had walls that were finished by weaving twigs back and forth over the outer poles that held up the roof. The spaces between the twigs were filled up with a plaster made of mud. Walls like this are called *wattle and daub* walls.

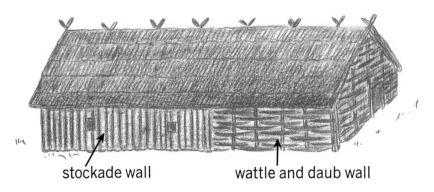

stockade wall   wattle and daub wall

An ancient farmhouse

17

Houses in Ancient Egypt

The Nile River gave ancient Egypt many gifts. It made a fertile valley in which Egyptians have farmed for thousands of years. Its mud was used as a building material. The reeds, *papyrus* (puh-PY-rus) plants and palms that grew along the river were used for building, too. The cliffs through which the Nile cuts its channel gave Egypt her building stone.

Egyptian houses of 6,000 years ago were one-room circular huts of wattle and daub. The wattle was a mesh made of river reeds. The daub was river mud. Often the huts had porches with roofs held up by columns made of reeds that had been tied in bundles.

Later houses were somewhat larger and were rectangular in shape. Corner posts were made by tying papyrus stalks together. Bundles of papyrus stalks also served as columns for porch roofs. Single papyrus stalks were placed between the corner posts, making the framework for wattle and daub walls. The walls were plastered with mud both inside and outside and were painted in bright colors after they had dried. Beams of bundled papyrus stalks or palm trunks were laid across the top of the walls to make a flat roof. A matting of reeds was placed over the beams. The matting was then plastered with a thick coat of mud. When the mud dried, it became very hard and strong. Because there was almost no rain in Egypt, these mud roofs held up very well. They were used as outdoor living quarters. Small houses had outdoor stairways leading up to the roofs. Large houses had inside stairways.

The houses that were built in Egypt about 2,500 years ago were built of mud that had been shaped into bricks and allowed to dry in the sun. Sun-dried bricks are called *adobe* (uh-DOE-bee).

Houses of very rich people were sometimes made of stone, with stone columns to hold up their porch roofs. The corners of these stone houses were carved to look like the bundles of papyrus stalks used as corner posts in the earlier wattle and daub houses. The stone columns were carved, too, to look like the bundled reed or papyrus columns that held up the porch roofs of the earlier mud houses.

Columns carved to look like papyrus and palm leaves

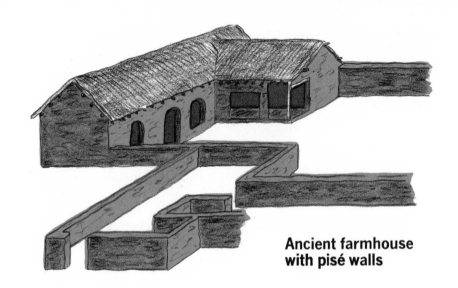

**Ancient farmhouse
with pisé walls**

Houses of Ancient Mesopotamia

Mesopotamia, the country now known as Iraq, had neither building stone nor timber trees. But Mesopotamia had two great rivers, the Tigris and the Euphrates. Reeds and palm trees grew along their banks. River mud and clay were plentiful. So reeds, clay and river mud were the chief building materials of ancient Mesopotamia.

Nomads were the first people who lived in Mesopotamia. They built woven reed huts. Huts like this are still built by Arabs who live in the marshes of southern Iraq.

The first permanent houses were built about 7,000 years ago. They were made of pounded clay. Clay is a kind of earth that sticks together easily. Pounded clay is

20

called *pisé* (pee-ZAY). The pounded clay was piled into baskets. Basketfuls of pisé were dumped on top of each other. This is how crude pisé walls were built. They had to be made very thick to stand up well. Roofs were made in the same way that the Egyptians made their roofs. Because there was so little timber, the roof beams were very short. As a result, rooms were very narrow. These early permanent houses had many long narrow rooms that were separated by thick pisé walls. The rooms were usually grouped around an open courtyard. The hearth for cooking was often in the courtyard.

Houses of clay bricks were first built about 5,500 years ago. To make a clay brick, first earth containing clay was mixed with a little chopped straw or dung. The straw or dung kept the brick from cracking or changing its shape. Then water was added to the mixture and stamped in thoroughly. The clay mud was then put into a wooden frame to shape it. The frame was taken off while the brick was still wet. The clay bricks were left in the sun to dry. Bricks are still made in this way in parts of Western Asia.

About 5,000 years ago the Mesopotamians began to dry bricks by baking them in *kilns*. Kiln-dried bricks are much stronger than sun-dried bricks. Using kiln-dried bricks, the ancient builders of Mesopotamia began to make *arches* and *vaulted* roofs. This is the first time they were ever made.

Houses of Ancient Greece

Timber and stone for building were plentiful in ancient Greece. So besides using sun-dried bricks and mud plaster for building, the Greeks used wood and stone, too.

The earliest Greek houses, of about 2,500 B.C. (this was about 4,500 years ago), were one-room circular huts. By about 1,700 B.C. Greek houses had become rectangular in shape. Some of these houses had walls made of small stones that were held together by mortar. Other houses were of *half-timber* construction. Half-timber houses were made in this way: Heavy wooden beams were placed at equal distances from each other, standing *vertically* or straight up. The spaces between the vertical beams were filled with a lath made of twisted twigs or reeds. The lath was completely covered with a heavy coat of mud plaster. So a half-timber wall was part timber and part wattle and daub. The timber beams were left uncovered. Roofs were flat. They were made very much the way Egyptian flat roofs were made.

Any house in which wooden posts and beams form a frame to which the roof and outside walls are attached is called a *frame house*. A half-timber house is one type of frame house. Other types of frame houses, built much later, are described on pages 40 to 45.

The Greeks did not use arches for building. They were

able to build very large rooms by using long wooden beams or slabs of marble to hold up the roof. The long beams or slabs of marble were, in turn, held up by rows of columns.

Some houses had inner gardens surrounded by a row of columns. Some houses had upper stories and basements. Foundations were usually of stone. Floors were made of heavy wooden timbers, which fitted into grooves in the stone foundation.

A typical large rectangular house was the *megaron* (MEH-guh-ron) house. The megaron was a large central living room. Its roof was supported by four central columns arranged in a square. The columns surrounded the hearth.

Two small rectangular Greek houses

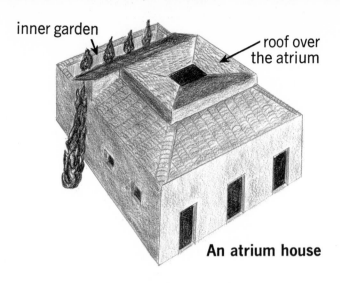

inner garden

roof over
the atrium

An atrium house

Ancient Roman Houses

By the year 140 B.C. (this was about 2,100 years ago) most of Italy had been conquered by the city of Rome. The Romans had conquered Greece and Spain, too. As a result the building styles of the Romans began to resemble the building styles of the people they conquered.

The Romans sometimes built with stone and wood, but they built mostly with brick and *concrete.* They made concrete by mixing together sand, small stones and a cement called *pozzolana* (pot-suh-LON-uh). Pozzolana was made from the ashes that came out of volcanoes. The Romans knew how to use bricks to build arches and vaults.

The earliest Italian houses that we know anything about were small rectangular huts built before the Romans ruled Italy. Each hut had a central kitchen-living room with a hearth in the middle. There was a hole in the roof of the hut to let the smoke out. These houses were usually built of stone.

Early Roman houses were also built around a central hall. But these houses had a separate room that served as a kitchen. Nevertheless, the Romans still built a hole in the roof over the central hall even though it was not needed to let smoke out. Even so, the hall was named after the smoke-blackened living room of the early hut. It was called *atrium* (AY-tree-um), from the Latin word "ater" that means black. The hole in the roof of the atrium house was used to let in rain water. The water collected in a pool and then drained into a cistern where it was stored. This was the early Roman's water supply.

Pompeii and Herculaneum were Roman cities near the volcano, Vesuvius. In the year A.D. 79, Vesuvius suddenly became active. Pompeii and Herculaneum were buried under the ashes that poured out of the mouth of the volcano. The cities were forgotten for about 1,600 years until they were discovered by accident. Since then the buildings in these cities have been uncovered very carefully. That is how we know what the houses of Pompeii and Herculaneum looked like.

The typical house of Pompeii had an atrium and many rooms leading off from it. It also had an inner garden with a Greek-style porch having many columns. The bedrooms usually led off from this inner court. The roof

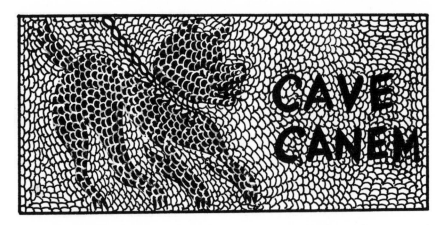

sloped gently and was tiled. Floors were often decorated with *mosaics* (moh-ZAY-iks), pictures made out of small colored stones and tiles. If the house had a watchdog, the entrance hall had a mosaic like the one on this page. *Cave canem* (CAH-weh CON-em) means "beware of the dog" in Latin.

Houses in the large cities were quite different. Rome had grown very fast. Land was very expensive. So, in order to provide housing for the largest number of people, apartment houses were built. The Roman apartment houses were owned by rich people who rented their apartments to the working people. In order to make a lot of money from rent, the owners built the houses four or even six stories high. Each floor was divided into many apartments with tiny rooms. These early Roman apartment buildings, called *insulae* (IN-syou-lee), were long and narrow. They were usually only two rooms deep. They were so poorly built that the Roman poet Juvenal said that they "shook with every gust of wind that blew." The owners of the insulae hardly ever repaired them. The apartments were unheated and overcrowded. Many rooms had no windows. Even though the buildings were many stories high, they had no inside toilets. These apartment houses were the world's first *slums*.

At the same time, there were Roman apartment houses that were very fine. In Ostia, a seaport near Rome, and in Herculaneum, the apartment houses were occupied by rich people. These apartments had large rooms with many windows. They had bathrooms with hot and cold running water and they had indoor toilets. Some apartments had outdoor balconies. Some apartments were even *duplex*, with rooms on two different floors connected by a stairway inside the apartment.

A duplex apartment house in Ostia

A large house built in Belgium by the Romans

Roman Houses in Northern Europe

By the year 200 the Romans had conquered England, France and Belgium. The Romans could not build out of concrete in these places because there was no pozzolana for making concrete. Even though building timber was plentiful they built their houses with stone or brick walls. They made their porch columns out of wood, however. Houses had sloping roofs to shed rain and snow. The Romans preferred to use tile to cover their roofs. However, they also used wooden shingles, flat stones and even *thatch*, a roof covering made of straw or reeds. Large Roman houses in these northern countries were centrally heated by an underground furnace. Stone-lined passageways carried hot air from the furnaces to every room.

Tower Houses

During the next few hundred years Rome was conquered by other peoples. There was constant fighting going on. The fall of Rome and the constant fighting brought about changes in the style of houses and the way in which they were built. Now smaller houses were almost always built out of wood. Wooden buildings could be built cheaply and quickly. The constant fighting made it necessary for people to build walls around their settlements. But a town surrounded by a wall cannot spread out. So the houses in these walled towns were tall and narrow. These *tower houses* were two or three stories high, with one or two rooms on each floor. The lower floor often had stone walls. The upper floor was often half-timber. The sloping roof was tiled. Windows in the upper floors had the shape of arches, carved to look like the stone arches of ancient Rome.

Tower houses

Castle and Farmhouse

Just as towns had to protect themselves because of their constant fear of being attacked, landowners had to find a way to protect themselves, too.

About 1,000 years ago the farmland of Europe was owned by rich lords. The farmers who worked the land were not free to leave it, but they could not own it. They paid for the use of the land with crops they grew or by doing work for the lord. The lords and their servants lived in strong stone castles in which they could defend themselves and fight back when they were attacked. The main part of a castle was a large tower called the *keep.* The keep was many stories high. The people who occupied the castle lived in the keep when the castle was under attack. The keep could not be heated by a central hearth, because it had more than one floor. It was heated, instead, by fireplaces. There was a fireplace on each floor. A great hood over the fireplace carried the smoke to a chimney.

The farmers who worked the land lived in villages that grew up along roads or paths. The early German farmhouse of this period had a single rectangular room that sheltered both the family and its domestic animals. The house was of half-timber construction. It had a steep thatched roof. The beds were built-in bunks. There was a central hearth. There were usually some built-in storage

A castle. The large round tower is the keep.

cabinets, a table and a few chairs. Sometimes there was a partition to separate the part of the room where people lived from the part that served as a stable. Windows were small. They were either protected by wooden shutters that could be closed or they were covered by oiled linen or oiled skins that let the light through.

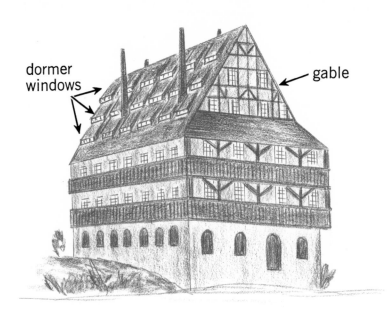

dormer windows

gable

German and Dutch Town Houses — 1400 to 1600

Land in towns was expensive. So houses were built on long, narrow strips of land. Usually the narrow end of a house faced the street. The houses sometimes were six stories high. They had steep roofs. In the walled towns of the German Alps the roofs were so tall and steep that the upper two or three stories were inside the roof.

Some German houses were built with the roof ridge-pole *parallel* or in the same direction as the street. These houses were often built with *dormer windows*. The family wash was hung inside the dormer for easy indoor drying. These town houses were often of half-timber construction. The timbers were decorated with carvings.

Some town houses of Holland and Germany were built with the ridgepole at right angles to the street. Then the pointed end or *gable* of the house faced the street. Houses that were built of brick were made more interesting looking by making the gable look like a staircase. Sometimes a hoist was attached to the top of the gable for lifting things from the ground to the upper stories.

Glass was now being used for windows. However, only small panes of glass could be made. So large windows were divided into small sections by vertical dividers called *mullions* (MULL-yuns) and horizontal dividers called *transoms* (TRAN-sums). The small sections of the windows are called *lights*. The windows had straight tops, so that they could be opened and closed easily.

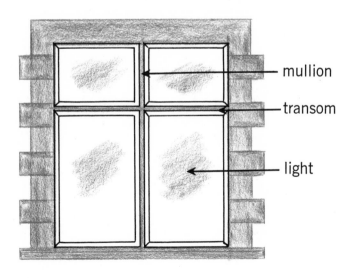

mullion

transom

light

England: Stone and Half-timber Buildings

Tourists who drive through the English countryside usually visit the Cotswold Hills (COT-swold). They drive on to Stratford-on-Avon where Shakespeare lived about 350 years ago. In this part of England people still live in houses that are hundreds of years old. The houses are still in very good condition because they were built very carefully.

The Cotswold houses are usually built of a fine building stone that is found in this region. The houses have steep gabled roofs covered with thin slabs of Cotswold stone, known as "stone slates." Each "stone slate" used

for roofing first had a hole drilled near one end. Then the "slate" was nailed to the roof boards with an oak peg. The Cotswold houses often have dormer windows. Their window panes are very small. The stone walls of these houses are between 18 inches and two feet thick. The houses are heated by fireplaces. There may be a fireplace in each of the main rooms of the house. Chimneys are of "stone slate," too. The Cotswold houses are beautifully finished on the inside. Wooden moldings are often carved. The plaster ceilings often have beautiful decorations.

There are still half-timber houses in many parts of England. The picture on page 34 shows how the timber frame was built. Nails were not used for joining the timber because iron was scarce.* *Mortise* (MORE-tus) and *tenon* (TEN-un) joints‡ and wooden pegs held the beams tightly together.

Until about 300 years ago most of the houses of London were half-timber. In the year 1666 there was a great fire in that city. More than 13,000 houses were burned. Since then frame construction is no longer allowed in London. Most towns in England do not allow the building of timber-framed houses either.

* See Learning About Steel Through The Story of a Nail by the same authors. The John Day Company, 1961.
‡ See *Tools in Your Life* by Irving Adler. The John Day Company, 1956.

England: Brick Factory Houses

As more and more land in England was cleared for farming, a shortage of wood for building developed. Stone was still used wherever there was building stone nearby. Elsewhere, brick began to be used more and more, since clay for brickmaking was found all over England. By 1800 brick had become the most common building material for walls.

At about that time, factories had appeared all over England. Factories employed many workers who had to live near their place of work. Buildings to house the workers were built by the factory owners.

The English factory owners were no different from the rich Romans who built the insulae. They wanted to make as much money as they could. So they built cheap houses. Because brick was the cheapest building material, they built the houses of brick. They crowded as many houses as they could into a small space. So they built two rows of houses back to back. Each house had four rooms on a floor. But the back two rooms had no light.

Sanitary conditions in these rows of brick houses were very poor. There were no garbage collections, so people threw their garbage into the street. The apartments did not have private toilets. *Privies* (PRIH-vees), toilets without water for flushing, were in the cellars. Houses were so crowded that sometimes as many as 200 people used one privy. Often there were pigsties in the cellars, too. The pigs dug around in the garbage that littered the streets. Many houses had no water nearby for drinking or washing. The people who lived in these houses would go from door to door in the richer neighborhoods, begging for water. Because of the filth and overcrowding, there was much sickness in these factory dwellings. This is what English factory slums were like in the nineteenth century.

A nineteenth-century London slum

Pueblos in Taos, New Mexico. The objects shaped like igloos are ovens.

The Pueblo: The First American Apartment House

Even before the white men came to America, there were apartment houses there. They were the houses of the Pueblo (PWEH-blow) Indians, who lived in what is now Arizona and New Mexico. Their houses are called *pueblos*. The Pueblo Indians were farmers. So they built permanent houses. They were always in danger of being attacked by other Indian tribes. So they built houses that were easy to defend.

Pueblo villages were built either against steep slopes or in narrow river gorges. The walls of the first pueblos were made of pisé and then plastered smooth with clay. In later years adobe was used instead of pisé. The roofs of the pueblos were flat.

Each family lived in one room. These one-room houses were built next to each other, with no space between them. To make it easier to protect, the pueblo had no windows and was entered through an opening in the roof, which was reached by a ladder. The ladder was pulled up if the pueblo was attacked.

As the pueblo villages became crowded, there was no room for them to stretch out in a line. So new houses were built on top of the old ones. They were set back a little so that they looked like steps. The floors of the new houses were the roofs of the old ones. The upper-level houses did not have to be entered through the roof. Pueblos were often six stories high. Later pueblos had windows.

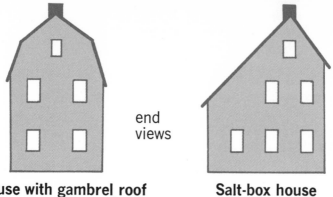

end views

House with gambrel roof   **Salt-box house**

Houses in Early America

Just as children usually look like their parents, the houses the early American settlers built looked like the houses in the countries from which they came.

The Spaniards who first settled in Mexico built houses with ribbed vaults and beautiful ironwork like the houses of Spain. The Puritans who settled in New England built houses in half-timber style. The eighteenth-century English settlers of Boston and Philadelphia built neat brick houses that looked like the better brick houses of London at that time. The Dutch who settled along the Hudson River built stone houses that were like the Dutch houses they had left behind.

At the same time that the settlers were copying the houses they were used to, they were also changing them. The Spanish priests who built churches among the Indians of the Southwest used Indian labor. So their churches began to look more and more like the simple dwellings of the Indians. The Puritans found that the strong New England winds seeped into every crack of their half-timber houses. So they began to cover their outside walls with *clapboard* (KLAA-burd). Clapboards are long boards that are thicker at one edge than at the other. They are nailed on one above the other so that they overlap. This helps make the walls windproof. Now that the timbers were covered by clapboards, it was no longer necessary to fill the spaces between the timbers with wattle and daub. But it was necessary to have more vertical posts to which to nail the clapboards. So light vertical posts, called *studs,* replaced the wattle and daub between the timbers.

The need for more space changed the shape of some of these early American houses. In parts of New England, when additional space was needed in a house, rooms were added to the lower floor at the back. Then the roof had to be extended so that it covered these added rooms. This is how the *salt-box* style of New England house developed.

The Dutch found they had to change the shape of their houses when they started building wider houses. If they wanted to use the attic as a room, the sloping roof which formed the walls of the attic would have to be steep. A steep roof on a wide house would have to be very high. To save wood the Dutch made the upper part of the roof less steep than the lower part. A roof like that is called a *gambrel* (GAM-bruhl) roof.

The Balloon Frame House

The population of the United States began to grow very quickly during the nineteenth century. Settlers kept moving westward as the country became more crowded. Many settlers first built temporary dwellings, which could be built quickly and cheaply. They built timber and earth *dugouts*, like those of the ancient Russian mammoth hunters, or *log cabins*. Later they built permanent frame houses.

It took a lot of work by skillful carpenters to build a wooden house because the joining was done using wooden pegs and handmade joints. Although the United States had plenty of timber for building, it didn't have enough skilled carpenters to build the houses that were needed. Luckily, the machine-made steel nail and the *balloon frame* house were invented at about this time. Machine-made steel nails were cheap. So they replaced wooden pegs and handmade joints in building.

The first clapboard houses used the studs only for holding up the clapboard and for filling the spaces between the heavy beams. The balloon frame house used no heavy beams at all. Instead, studs all cut to the same height were nailed to a piece of wood, called the *plate*, that rested on the foundation. Another plate was nailed across the top of the studs. Now the studs could be used to hold up the roof. If the studs were very long, a third plate could be nailed halfway up them. Then the studs could be used to hold up an upper floor. The clapboard on the outside of the house was nailed to the studs, too.

There are two other kinds of frame houses, the *braced frame* and *platform frame,* that are close relatives to the balloon frame.

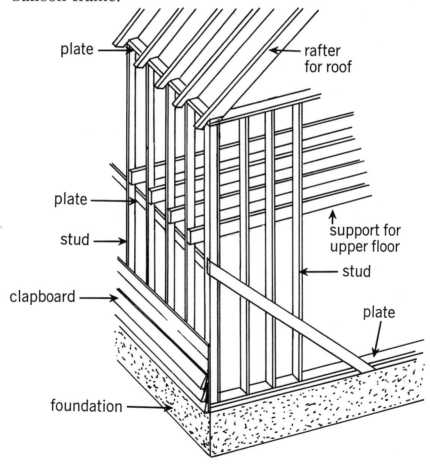

A balloon frame house

43

American Houses Today

Most small houses, in towns and rural areas of the United States, are of frame construction. The frames may be covered with a facing of brick, or they may be covered with clapboards, wood shingles, or stucco, a kind of cement put on like mud plaster. New materials have been developed, too, to cover the frame. Plywood, sheets of asbestos, and asphalt shingles are also used. Roofs may be covered with slate or with asbestos, asphalt or wooden shingles.

The greatest changes that have taken place in the houses people live in resulted from a number of discoveries and inventions that were made in the nineteenth century. Coal production increased and, at the same time, a cheap way of making good steel was invented. Oil and natural gas were discovered and a way of making illuminating gas was developed. Most important of all, ways of using electricity were developed.

The modern house is heated centrally by a coal, oil or gas furnace. Heat is piped to every room of the house. The modern house has indoor toilets and bathrooms with hot and cold running water. The water is heated by coal, oil, gas or electricity. Water pumps are powered by electricity. The modern house has either a gas or electric stove for cooking. It is lighted at night by electricity. It may have many appliances, usually run by electricity or gas, that make the work of the modern housewife easier. It may have an automatic washing machine and a clothes dryer. It may have an electric automatic dish washer. It has a refrigerator run by either gas or electricity. Furnaces, pipes, refrigerators, stoves and home appliances are all made from steel.

The modern house has made life easier for the people who live in it. As a result they have more time for recreation.

A modern American house for older people

45

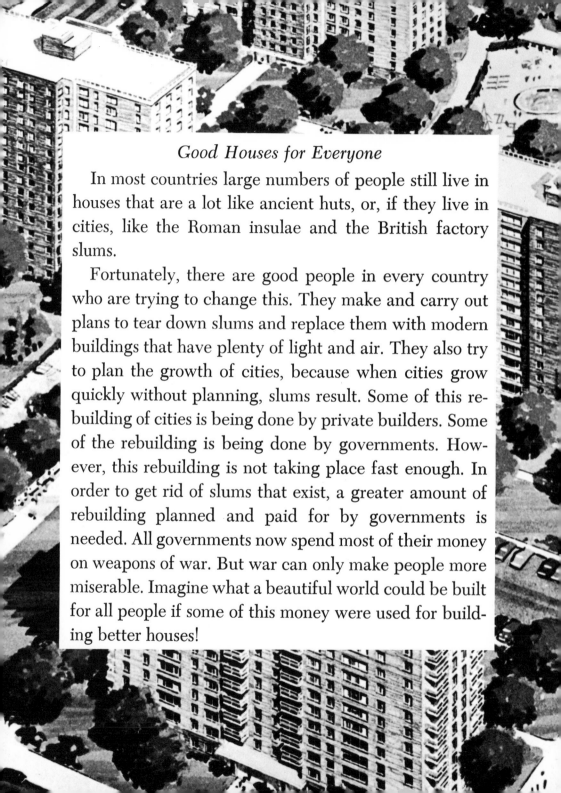

Good Houses for Everyone

In most countries large numbers of people still live in houses that are a lot like ancient huts, or, if they live in cities, like the Roman insulae and the British factory slums.

Fortunately, there are good people in every country who are trying to change this. They make and carry out plans to tear down slums and replace them with modern buildings that have plenty of light and air. They also try to plan the growth of cities, because when cities grow quickly without planning, slums result. Some of this rebuilding of cities is being done by private builders. Some of the rebuilding is being done by governments. However, this rebuilding is not taking place fast enough. In order to get rid of slums that exist, a greater amount of rebuilding planned and paid for by governments is needed. All governments now spend most of their money on weapons of war. But war can only make people more miserable. Imagine what a beautiful world could be built for all people if some of this money were used for building better houses!

Index

ABOUT THE AUTHORS

IRVING and RUTH ADLER have written more than 50 books about science and mathematics. Dr. Adler has been an instructor in mathematics at Columbia University and at Bennington College, and was formerly head of the mathematics department of a New York City high school. Mrs. Adler, who formerly taught mathematics, science and art in schools in the New York area, recently also taught at Bennington. In addition to working with her husband writing this book, she has joined with him on 19 other titles in the *Reason Why* series and drawn the illustrations for most of them as well as for many other books written by him.

Books by Irving Adler alone and books by him in collaboration with Ruth Adler have been printed in 77 different foreign editions, in 10 languages and in 9 reprint editions.

The Adlers now live in the country in Shaftsbury Township, near Bennington, Vermont.